HER COMPLICATED LOVE

Her Complicated Love

TAMEKA CUMMINGS

Charleston, SC
www.PalmettoPublishing.com

Her Complicated Love
Copyright © 2023 by Tameka Cummings

All rights reserved
No portion of this book may be reproduced, stored in a retrieval system, or transmitted in any form by any means—electronic, mechanical, photocopy, recording, or other—except for brief quotations in printed reviews, without prior permission of the author.

First Edition

Paperback ISBN: 979-8-8229-1728-6
eBook ISBN: 979-8-8229-1729-3

CONTENTS

Chapter 1	1
Chapter 2	5
Chapter 3	13
Chapter 4	17
Chapter 5	23
Chapter 6	28
Chapter 7	32
Chapter 8	35
Chapter 9	39
Chapter 10	42
Chapter 11	46
Chapter 12	50
Chapter 13	53
Chapter 14	58
Chapter 15	61
Chapter 16	66
Chapter 17	71

Chapter 1

She's beautiful and smart. She's kind and funny. She's compassionate, with a pure heart. She has pure love but sometimes feisty. She's spontaneous and humble. She's strong but has a weakness. She's hardworking but has little patience. She's loved by her friends and family but sometimes lonely. She's ambitious and knows exactly what she wants. She's selfish when it comes to her heart. She knows pain, and she knows love. She's protective when it comes to the ones she loves. She's caring and deserving of respect. She's grateful and optimistic. She's confused and has some complicated issues entangled in her heart. She's energetic but tired at times. She wants to be free but loved. She wants what the heart wants but doesn't want to hurt anybody.

She's a lover and a friend. She's a wife and a mother. She loves her family, but she loves him too. She's a caregiver and a wonderful friend. She's playful and sometimes chill. She's mindful at times and very religious. She makes mistakes and tries to learn from them. It's hard for her to say "no" at times. She's very trusting—until her trust is broken. She's full of hope and desires complete joy. She sometimes plays it safe and likes honesty, no matter how hard it will hurt. She wants to be supported and feel significant.

She's beautiful and sexy. She's fun filled and her light radiant beyond the skies. She's wholesome and creative. She's a great cook and wants validation. She's sexual but prefers gentleness in the bedroom. She likes date nights and to be shown attention. She likes and deserves to be pampered sometimes. She's funny at times but serious most of the time. She's an awesome woman but needs to figure herself out. She doesn't want to hurt anyone, and she doesn't want to get hurt. She tries to be healthy and take care of herself. She's very forgiving but doesn't forget. She desires to be a priority. She wants to feel seen by others. She desires approval. She's sick of being tired. She's willing to try and make it work, but she wants to give up as well. She loves unconditionally. She embraces love. She supports the ones she loves, and she is always there when needed. She's terrified of being alone. She wants to feel protected and accepted by the one she loves. This girl's name is Ava.

She has desired a relationship with her father ever since she was old enough to say, "Daddy." She has desired a father figure in her life. Her father failed her, and the other one failed her too. Ava had a dad who raised her, and she had a dad who helped create her. She never met her biological father. The step-in dad started out good but let drugs take him over. She needed his love and so wanted it. She didn't know early on that her "dad" wasn't her biological father. Her dad loved her, but when he got mad, he would bring up the other man to Ava's mother "Maura". Ava was too young to understand what the fussing was about. She thought her parents were happy and in love. This wasn't really the case. Ava's mom was broken and had a history of picking broken men. However, Ava found out years later that her mom had been pregnant with her when she met her brothers' dad. This was the only father she knew. The love and affection from her dad was what she wanted and needed. Instead of getting this love from her dad or the other guy, she sought it from the guys who came into her life.

Ava loved hard and wanted these guys to love her back in the same way she cared for them. Ava didn't know what real love looked like. She didn't really know what a real man looked like. She only knew brokenness. Her mom was broken, and her dad was broken. Moreover, her biological dad was broken. Ava wanted to find out information on her biological dad, thinking that he was a hero and that he would one day come save her and be the dad that she needed. Ava later found out that he was even more broken than the parents she had.

Ava's biological dad came from a broken home. His dad murdered his mother in front of him. His dad went to prison, and he was raised by his aunt. His aunt raised him the best she could under the circumstances, but he still became a troubled kid who later turned into a troubled adult. Ava held on to the thought of him being a good man until she found out different. Ava had a friend who researched her biological dad, and she found out he died the same day as her mom. Ava wanted to meet him, but she never got the chance to. Her friend also found the woman he was married to. She looked this up later and found out that she moved here from Maryland and was living right here in her state. She got in touch with her biological dad's widow, and they did lunch and talked. This lady brought pictures, and they both chatted. Ava found out she really didn't miss out on having him in her life. He was worse off than the one who partially raised her. Ava did keep in contact with his wife because she could tell she was a good person. Ava still didn't get what she really wanted from the dad in her life, so she sought it through the relationship choices throughout her life.

Chapter 2

Ava had met quite a few guys in her past. She didn't have too many relationships, but she did sleep with a few guys. Ava tried to date and be versatile. Most of the time, she just wanted to have some fun. She was an Aries and enjoyed the thrill of first dates and meeting someone for the first time. Ava was very adventurous, and she enjoyed talking, dancing, and going out with her friends. Ava was also a homebody. She enjoyed spending time alone as well. Ava met her very first boyfriend, Cole while in high school. The thrilling part about Cole was that he was older. Cole was a social butterfly and he was loveable and carefree. However, Cole was a bad boy. Among being handsome, Cole was dangerous. Ava fell for Cole pretty quickly. Things moved quite fast with the two. He was older than she and was not attending school. Cole had his own car and almost seemed to have his stuff together…until he didn't.

Ava enjoyed the experience of being with Cole picking her and her cousins up from school. She enjoyed having her friends at school, but she also enjoyed being with Cole and his friends after school or weekends. While Ava was finishing up her last year of high school, Ava met another guy by the name of Luke who caught her eye. Luke was younger than her. He had a swag about him. He was the total opposite of her older boyfriend, at least she thought he was. Luke was very handsome, smart, athletic, and a little more laid back than Cole. Ava wouldn't give this young man the time of day at first, but she enjoyed him chasing her. Besides, Luke was two years younger than she. Ava had a boyfriend who was two years older. What could this young boy offer her? Ava really enjoyed Luke chasing her. It gave her the attention she so desired. On the other hand, Ava had this older boyfriend Cole who protected her but she had someone who admired her and really wanted to get to know her better.

Ava's relationship was going well with Cole until he skipped town. He left town for a few months without saying a word to Ava. Cole was into selling drugs and other criminal activity, so she assumed something must have happened to him. This saddened Ava because she thought he just abandon her. Ava was confused by what happened with Cole. She assumed he abandoned her just as her dad did. At that point, Ava decided to move on with her life. She finally gave Luke a chance. Luke desired to have a relationship with Ava. Ava was attracted to him physically and she loved his swag. Ava liked Luke's style. It was something about him that really caught her eye at first. Besides, Luke made Ava feel wanted.

Ava still had feelings for Cole and was confused about both these guys. Luke tried really hard to make her fall for him, and she finally did. Besides, what did she have to loose, Cole had left her so she was single again. Ava adored Luke but she didn't want to hurt him. Ava knew this love for Luke was new for him. Ava knew she might have been Lukes first. Luke was sweet and everything Cole wasn't. Cole didn't treat Ava bad but he didn't have a romantic bone in his body. Luke was the opposite. He wanted to take Ava out and do things with her as a couple. Ava felt that Luke was falling hard for her. In addition, having sex with him for the first time didn't make it better. Luke was more in love with Ava. She cared for him back, but didn't want to hurt him. She enjoyed spending time with Luke. She really loved his mother. Things were going really good and then something changed.

Cole had returned home. He wanted things to pick up where they had left off, but Ava was confused. She still loved Cole but she also cared for Luke. Ava didn't know what to do. She couldn't tell Cole she had moved on. Moreover, she didn't want to hurt Luke either. What was a girl to do? Ava decided to tell Luke that Cole was back in town. She knew Cole wouldn't let her go that easily. Besides, he was a bad boy. He was into the streets, and he got a thrill out of fighting and causing trouble. She didn't want him to hurt Luke because she did care for him. So Ava decided to break up with Luke. He didn't take the news well. He wasn't letting Ava go without a fight. Again, what was a girl to do? During this time Luke was changing. He was in the streets even more. He was becoming more like Cole. Ava liked Luke as he was and she didn't want him to change. Part of her thought he may have changed because of her.

Ava tried again to break things off with Luke but he wasn't having it. So, Ava and Luke had an agreement with one another. She decided to stay with him as well, but she made him promise not to come around when Cole was in the area. Ava had her own transportation, so she was able to pull things off by seeing them both. Her younger boyfriend would stop by her job right before her older boyfriend would be leaving. Sometimes they even passed each other but didn't know each other. Ava was scared and afraid at times. She was living a secret life that was starting to overwhelm her. She tried once again to break it off with Luke, but he would threaten to go to Cole if she broke up with him. Ava stayed with them both. She was stressed to the limit. However, she did get a thrill out of living a double life. Ava was an Aries so this excited her at times.

During a slip up with Cole, Ava became pregnant, but she knew who the father was. She always used protection with Luke, but had that slip up with Cole. Ava kept a calendar of the days she had sex with these two guys. Ava never slept with them on the same days. She may have mess with one on a Tuesday and the other on a Saturday. but never in the same day or back to back. Now that Ava was pregnant, she really wanted her family to work out. She wanted to make things work with Cole but she was scared to tell him the truth about her double life she had been living.

In addition, during Ava's pregnancy, Luke always wondered whether the baby was his or not. She assured him it wasn't. She didn't want to hurt him, but she wanted to give her family a chance; besides, she never really had a real family. Ava came from brokenness. She always wanted to feel complete. She wanted something she really never had growing up, and that was a happy home. But how could her home be happy when she was in love with two guys at the same time? Was this even possible? Could she possibly be in love with two guys at the same time? Well, she felt like it was love.

Ava was only seventeen at the time. Did she even really know what love was? It's hard to say. At least she thought she did.

Ava once again didn't know what she would do. Cole even proposed to her. Ava wasn't ready for marriage. Moreover, as she matured and really got to know him, she didn't want to live that dangerous life anymore with Cole either. Ava thought she felt safe with Cole because he always protected her, but as she got a little older, she became scared. Ava became scared of the person Cole was becoming. He was mean but not to her. He did stuff that would get him in trouble. While she was with him one day, he decided to go and beat up his cousin's ex-boyfriend because he hit his cousin. Well, the cousin's ex-boyfriend's dad and brother came out the door and started shooting their guns. They didn't care whom they hit at the time. The cousin and Ava were in the car, and Cole had been shot. His cousin had to drive him and Ava to the hospital. Ava was scared out of her mind. He was bleeding out everywhere, and she was afraid she was going to lose him. Ava was also about to have a baby. She didn't want to have to raise her child on her own. This was stressing Ava out. This life was something she didn't want to have to deal with anymore. She knew Cole was in the streets and that he was about that life, but Ava didn't want this for her child.

Ava gave birth to a healthy baby boy, Zane. Cole and Ava's mom, Maura were there when she delivered. She still had some hard feelings against her mother because her mother didn't want her to have the baby. Ava's mother felt this baby would ruin her life. Ava's mom also didn't want her seeing Cole either, because she knew what it was like being a young mother and in a relationship with a bad boy. Ava's mother didn't make good choices when it came to men, either, so it was kind of hard for Ava to take the advice of her mother.

Ava just thought her mother wanted to see her unhappy. However, when Ava's mother laid eyes on Zane, she was in love with him. She adored that baby and wanted nothing but to be the best grandmother that she could be, even though she was still young herself.

Ava's mother, Maura did everything for baby Zane. Maura made sure Zane had everything he needed. Maura kept Zane while Ava worked but refused to babysit on the weekend. Besides, Ava's mom was still young. She still partied and went out with her friends on the weekend. Ava had to grow up really fast. She still saw Luke after giving birth to Zane from time to time. She spent time with both Cole and Luke at different times. On the weekends, she and her best friend would go hang out with Luke and his friends. Ava would have baby Zane with her as well. Luke didn't mind because he treated baby Zane as if he were his. Ava constantly reminded him that that was not his child. He didn't care; he just loved her and the baby. Ava's older boyfriend, Cole got deeper into the streets, and those streets consumed him. He eventually got arrested for something that got him locked away for some years. This devastated Ava because her child would have to grow up without his dad. She was hurt and angry with him at the same time. Ava was now a single mother. She had to put on her "big girl drawers" as the older folks used to say, and be the provider for her child and herself.

Ava had her own place and was determined to be a great mother and provider for her kid. Ava remained in a relationship with Luke, but he was changing as well. Luke started hanging with the wrong crowds. He started doing some of the things that Cole was doing. Ava tried talking with Luke, and she tried to convince him to stay in school and on track. By this time, Ava was out of school and Luke was close to finishing. She had no expectations of Luke to be a father to baby Zane, but she wanted Luke to do well for himself. He was young and had his whole life a head of him. Luke was smart and very talented. Luke could have made something great of himself and Ava really believed he could do that. Luke didn't listen, he just wanted fast money. Luke was selling drugs and doing other things that would eventually get him arrested as well. He started seeing other females; Ava wasn't going to put up with that. However, part of her wanted him to live his life though. Ava was finally ready to walk away from this relationship with Luke. The last night was a night to remember. Ava and Luke loved to make love off of Joe's "All that I am" album. Luke was really good in bed. He could last for a long time. The Album would play almost all the way through. Who knew that night would be the last time she saw Luke.

Ava decided she was ready to walk away from Luke. They had a great night but that was it for her. She wasn't going to allow Luke to control her in that way anymore because he had no one this time to tell. She was, in a way, happy he started seeing someone else because his mood and energy had changed. He started to feel as though he could talk to her anyway and they started arguing and fighting more. Neither seemed happy with one another, unless they were having sex. Luke spent more time with his friends than with Ava. Ava knew Luke wasn't ready to be a father or take on responsibility of being one, so deep down she knew it was time for him to move on. Things use to be exciting for them. Sex was great and they both were excited by one another earlier on, but things changed when life changed for them both. Ava and Luke had their last argument and mutually decided they both would walk away from the relationship. Ava was sadden by this because she cared for Luke and she knew he cared for her. Ava cried for 24 hours straight after Luke left. She grieved the relationship with Luke but realized that the timing was off for them. Besides, they both were young and needed to live their lives and find life outside of each other. Luke left that night and shortly after that night, Luke got into some mess and went to prison.

Chapter 3

Ava put these relationships behind her. She was ready to move on and live freely for a while. Ava wanted to date and have friends. She didn't want to be tied down anymore. She wanted her own independence and her space. She wanted sex sometimes but not anything too serious. Ava started enjoying her peace and independence. It was hard being a single woman because she had been in relationships the last few years of her life. Ava was finally proud of the woman she was becoming. Ava had goals and dreams. She had so much she wanted to do. With her mother, Maura behind and on her side, she felt she could do anything. Ava never had a relationship with her birth father, and she had a rocky relationship with her dad who raised her. Him being her dad would never change because she loved him. Although, Ava felt he chose drugs over her and her siblings. Ava always desired that father-daughter relationship but didn't get it. This was the same for Ava's sisters. They chose the wrong guys and looked for exactly what they didn't get from their dad. Ava wanted to move differently. She didn't want to focus on a man anymore. She wanted to work on herself and find herself.

Ava was working two jobs and doing really well raising Zane. Ava had help from both grandmothers. Her mom babysat during the weekdays, and her baby's father's mother kept her kid while she worked weekends at her second job. Ava felt good about life. Ava was dating a little. She was meeting different guys and having fun. She didn't want anything serious. Ava was there for a good time and not a long time. She didn't want to catch feelings. She didn't want to hurt anyone either. She just wanted to be honest and let these guys know she wanted to stay single. Ava was active and felt healthy. She loved the person she was. Sometimes she felt lonely at times, but that went away really fast. The thought of giving her complete self to someone else was buried in the back of her head, she wasn't ready for that.

Things took a turn for the worse for Ava and her family. Ava's mom started getting sick quite a bit. Moreover, her mother was going to the doctor, but she kept being misdiagnosed. Ava started feeling a little depressed because her and her mother finally started getting close again. She loved the relationship and friendship they gained over this last year. Ava was scared of losing her mom. She wanted her mom to be OK. She wanted them to be fine. Maura was proud of the accomplishments of Ava. She never told her how proud she was of her, but she did tell other people, who told Ava.

Furthermore, during this time, Ava was working her part-time job, and she met a young man by the name of Frank-Lucas. She never thought of it as something serious, but there was something about this young man that she couldn't put her finger on. He tried and tried to talk to her, but she wasn't ready for anything serious. Honestly, he wasn't ready for anything serious either. She knew she was dealing with things with her mother. She was also dealing with the issue with her biological dad. One of Ava's half siblings reached out to her and told her that her biological father was sick, and he wanted to see her. He lived in Maryland. He was sending a ticket for her to visit. They had a plan worked out, but Ava was worried about her mother. She had planned to go meet him and finally be able to get to meet this man she had so desired to meet one day.

While all this was going on, Ava was still curious to see who this young man was that would stop by her job every weekend. Her curiosity grew stronger, and her physical attraction to him grew strong. She looked forward to seeing him each weekend. She made him chase her a little, but she was interested; she just couldn't let him see how interested she was. Ava was very prideful. She wanted to play hard to get, and she liked the chase. She asked her friends about this young man and found out that they shared a mutual friend. This mutual friend was more like a brother to her. He gave her the okay to proceed with the mutual friend, but he was a little hesitant. At that point she should have walked away because the connection between her and this young man was powerful. Ava never felt anything like what she felt with him. She had been in love before but not like this. She had chemistry with this young man like no other. Ava had dated around and met different guys. The situation and feeling were different for her. He was a little different from the guys she dated before. He was handsome like Luke and Cole but something was just different about him. He had a smile that could light up an entire room. He was sexy to her. Ava enjoyed his deep tone. She enjoyed seeing him smile. His silky dark skin tone was so attractive to her. He was beautiful from head to toe. She loved his long locks. This young man mesmerized her. There was something about him that Ava couldn't pinpoint. She wanted to get to know him better, but she wasn't ready for a relationship.

Chapter 4

Ava didn't even know this young man, but she did give him her number. Later that same night he called her. She was finally able to put a name with his face. His name was Frank-Lucas. The two of them talked all night long and got to know each other a little better. Ava found out he stayed in the same town as she did. He lived with his mother. Ava had her own place. Ava told him she had a son, and he told her he had a daughter and son. Ava always said she would never be with a guy who had kids. She had her mind made up about this. However, she had a kid. Why should this be an issue with this guy?

Ava and Frank-Lucas planned to meet up. One night Ava went to pick Frank-Lucas up, and he came back to her house. Ava even cooked for him. During her dating moments, she never cooked for any of her dates. She really never saw any of those dates going anywhere. However, again, there was something about Frank-Lucas. Ava wanted him, and she felt he wanted her too. She thought at first it was a physical attraction, even though that was part of it, it was much more with him. She almost felt like he reminded her of her dad. At that point, she probably should have walked away but she didn't.

Ava had a weekend night off, and Frank-Lucas wanted to come see her. Zane was with his other grandmother. His grandmother mostly kept and spent time with Zane on the weekends. Ava and Frank-Lucas had such a physical attraction to each other. He wanted her, and she wanted him, so the two made plans to see each other. They finally did what they both wanted to do: sleep together. They didn't talk about it, but they both wanted it—at least Ava did. Ava fantasized about doing it with Frank-Lucas. She picked him up from his mom's house, and they went back to her house. The first time was very short—two seconds short. Frank-Lucas got up out the bed and went and sat on the porch. Ava got dressed and went out to find him smoking a cigarette with his head down. She asked him what happened and whether something was wrong. He told her he had come. Ava never had that experience before. She had guys who came very quickly during intercourse but not this quick. The old Ava would have driven him home immediately, but she didn't. She actually liked him.

Frank-Lucas told her this had never happened to him before. She was wondering, then, why it had happened with her. Frank-Lucas told her this was the best he'd ever had. Ava was shocked. She thought all women were all the same. She was young and had a little experience with sex, but she didn't understand where he was coming from with this information. This statement made Ava feel really good because she liked him and wanted to see more of him.

Ava decided that night to give it a go with Frank-Lucas again. He did better the second time. However, she didn't get an orgasm, but this wasn't unusual for her. Ava could count on one hand how many she ever received. Ava and Frank-Lucas enjoyed each other during that night. He rested with her, and she took him home the next morning. Ava felt something for this young man. She was ashamed to think that she could be in love with him. Besides, love at first sight wasn't a real thing, was it? But Ava did know she had some sort of connection with Frank-Lucas. The two spent more nights together, and sex got better with the two. Ava really enjoyed spending time with Frank-Lucas. The two spent time with their mutual friends. They even played cards together. The two of them enjoyed going out to clubs and dancing. Ava was starting to think this situation was going to go somewhere. Ava was actually happy. She didn't care about the rule of not being with a man who had kids. She also didn't care about living the single life because she would have chosen Frank-Lucas. His life situation wasn't what she was used to, but she would have worked with him.

Frank-Lucas was at Ava's home one night, and Ava's mom, Maura was there. The two met, and he was really respectful. Ava's mom thought he was handsome. Ava's mom didn't think it was anything long term because she knew her daughter. She knew Ava had some commitment issues and that she liked feeling free, so she didn't think much of the situation. Furthermore, her mom cooked for Frank-Lucas that night. Ava wasn't going to cook for him anymore. She said the next meal would have to be on him. Frank-Lucas didn't cook, but he did order dinner another night. Ava thought this was a start, but she wasn't fully convinced that he was really into her . Ava knew he was feeling her sexually, and she was feeling him. Things seemed almost too good to be true. What she didn't know was that this situation was going to change really soon. The two hung out and spent time together alone and with friends. Things just felt right between the two. Ava enjoyed spending time with Frank-Lucas, and she thought he enjoyed the time with her. The two didn't label their relationship. It seemed they were friends with benefits. These two had such physical, sexual, and emotional connections between them. They always had sex when together or around each other. They had deep conversations, but sex was always the first priority between these two.

Lo and behold, Frank-Lucas had secrets, and he had a past. As Ava got to know Frank-Lucas and the people who knew him, she learned things that she didn't like. Ava adored this young man but found it hard to get past his past. Frank-Lucas had two baby-mothers who were associates or "friends." Frank-Lucas had a shaky past, especially when it came to a lot of women. Ava wasn't used to this. She didn't like sharing a man that she thought was hers with no other woman, especially ones from her hometown. She hated his past and really wanted to keep their relationship a secret. Ava was embarrassed by Frank-Lucas's past. Remember, Ava was very prideful, and she had an image to uphold. She wanted to be the strong woman who looked like she had it together and wouldn't just fall for anyone. Frank-Lucas had a way with the ladies. He was smooth, and that smile would just turn women on. Ava told herself she couldn't be with a guy like this. However, Ava was falling hard for Frank-Lucas. She hid how she really felt about him from her friends and family. She even hid it from him.

Frank-Lucas didn't really know how she felt at the time. Through all of this, Ava found out Frank-Lucas's past was catching up with him again. He had supposedly got another girl pregnant, and this was before he and Ava had gotten together. The girl was positive that it was his, but she was the "manufacturing ho, meaning she got around at the job." The child could have been anyone's. There were so many men this girl had messed with around the time she got pregnant. Again, Ava felt embarrassed because she wanted more from Frank-Lucas, but it seemed he didn't want it for himself. Ava tried to look past his past, but she couldn't. It was hard for her because every time she turned a corner, there was a girl he had been with. Ava wanted and needed better for herself. She couldn't picture being with a man like this. Frank-Lucas was a whore. He loved women, and it was easy for him to be with these women. Ava wondered why she had to fall for someone like Frank-Lucas. Ava wanted this to be a phase. She wanted to get over him and get on with her life.

It wasn't easy for Ava because she really had deep feelings for Frank-Lucas. Ava thought that with a little time, she could get over him. Ava was wrong. Ava prayed and prayed to get over Frank-Lucas. She even pulled away at times from their mutual friends, just so she didn't have to see Frank-Lucas. At times when she thought she was able to move on, he would show up with that smile and smooth tone, and she would fall all over again. Ava hated that. She hated the way Frank-Lucas made her feel. She hated that she loved him so deeply but could never be with someone like him. This really hurt Ava inside. She had an image she had to keep up. She had something to prove to her friends and family. She also didn't want Frank-Lucas to know how she felt about him because then he would have her exactly where he wanted her, at least, that is what she thought. Ava didn't want Frank-Lucas to know how she really felt. Ava would have rather been alone and heartbroken before letting Frank-Lucas know how she really felt. Inside, Ava was scared of what could have been between her and Frank-Lucas. Ava was also scared of rejection from him. She often wondered if he was as into her as she was into him. She knew there was something, but she just couldn't see exactly what it was between her and Frank-Lucas. Ava was an overthinker. She would make things up in her head that seemed right to her.

Chapter 5

Ava always assumed the worst when it came to Frank-Lucas. Ava couldn't be honest with Frank-Lucas or with herself. She wanted to be with him, but she just couldn't. Ava was complicated, and being with Frank-Lucas would be even more complicated for her. Frank-Lucas wasn't what she wanted or needed, but he was in her heart, mind, and soul. Ava felt love for Frank-Lucas on a different level. She almost thought that loving him was a punishment. She thought it was a punishment from her past relationship mistakes. Ava never felt this way about another guy. The love she experienced with Frank-Lucas was indescribable. She couldn't explain it to her friends, and she wouldn't explain it to them either. Ava felt Frank-Lucas's spirit even when he wasn't around. She relived their moments together, even when they were apart. Ava adored and desired to be with Frank-Lucas, but deep down inside, she just couldn't give her all to him. Ava prayed to God to get over him. She didn't see herself being with him long term; that was her reality.

Time had passed, and Frank-Lucas and Ava saw less of each other. Ava had started a new job and was looking to move soon. Frank-Lucas was doing him, and Ava was OK with it, as long as she didn't see it. Ava had bigger goals and dreams she wanted to pursue. She had responsibilities that Frank-Lucas neglected. For example, Ava was a full-time mom, and she worked full time. Frank-Lucas wasn't working at the time or taking care of his kids. Moreover, another kid was born, and the girl swore it was Frank-Lucas's kid. Ava didn't have time for the baby-mama drama. This young lady gave Ava hell. Frank-Lucas swore he wasn't dealing with this girl no more, but the way she taunted Ava, she begged to differ. Ava wasn't ready to be a stepmom to Frank-Lucas's kids or deal with the mothers of those other kids. Ava had other things on her mind. However, these things never allowed her to forget about Frank-Lucas. Ava told herself that Frank-Lucas was better left in her heart and mind than in her life at this time.

Frank-Lucas was spoiled. He was a mama's boy. He wasn't ready for what Ava was ready for. She wanted him to be, but deep down he wasn't mature enough for Ava. Ava went on with her life, and so did Frank-Lucas. She tried avoiding places he might be because she thought it would be easier for her to get over him. Ava stayed busy, trying to save money while working two jobs. She even applied for a few jobs out of the town she and Frank-Lucas resided in. Ava was serious about getting over him. But something happened that made Ava reconsider things. Ava's mother passed away, and soon as Frank-Lucas heard of the news, he reached out. Ava was almost over him; at least she thought she was—until seeing him again.

Ava couldn't deny the feelings and attraction she had for Frank-Lucas. Even during her grief, she wanted him. He felt so familiar to her. She wanted him, and she missed him so much. She wanted him to hug and kiss her. Ava wanted to make love to Frank-Lucas, and they did. She knew again that it wasn't what she needed, but it was everything at the time she wanted. Ava and Frank-Lucas picked up right where they left off as if no time had interrupted them. They went back into the friends-with-benefit stages that seemed too familiar to both of them.

Things got right back on track but fell off again. Ava still loved Frank-Lucas, and she felt Frank-Lucas loved her as well. However, it just wasn't great timing for them again. So the two had a conversation about what they wanted and needed, and Frank-Lucas made it very clear he wasn't ready for what Ava wanted. Ava respected his honesty because Frank-Lucas didn't really like expressing himself, but Ava loved it when he opened up to her. That was one of the things she felt attracted to him for: his openness. Once again, these two let things calm down, and they both went on their merry ways. Ava dated around with a few guys but nothing serious. Frank-Lucas messed around with a few girls, but again, it was nothing serious.

One day, Ava was coming home from a date and happened to see Frank-Lucas get out of a car with a girl that Ava was cool with. Lets say a friend of a friend. Ava couldn't even believe this. She was trying to move on from Frank-Lucas, but seeing him with this girl made her angry and jealous at the same time. The anger forced Ava to go across the street to their mutual friend's house and confront this girl and Frank-Lucas. Things really got heated. Ava tried to fight this girl, but she wouldn't fight Ava. Frank-Lucas didn't say anything. He smiled as if things were funny or as if this were a joke to him.

Ava hated Frank-Lucas at that moment. She hated this girl as well. She told this young lady that if she saw her anywhere, she was going to get her. Ava's mutual friends wouldn't let Ava get to this girl that night, but Ava was determined to get her. Frank-Lucas knew at that moment that Ava really cared for him and that he had hurt her. Ava wouldn't have cared if this was some random girl that he met and started seeing, but this girl was someone who hung out with Ava and their mutual friends. This girl had even stayed the night multiple times with Ava. Ava had had conversations with her about Frank-Lucas. This girl knew how Ava felt about Frank-Lucas. She knew some of Ava's and Frank-Lucas's darkest secrets. She even told Ava about the guy she was dealing with. Ava once liked this girl, but when this happened, she never wanted to see her again.

This situation really made Ava see life differently without Frank-Lucas. Ava was really ready to move on without Frank-Lucas. She knew things were over between them. She knew that she could never forgive Frank-Lucas for what he did to her.

Ava was embarrassed and hurt. She was ashamed of Frank-Lucas at this very moment. As much as she loved him, she hated him as well. Everything that she had tried to overlook from Frank-Lucas's past came to pass. This was the last straw for Ava. Even though she and Frank-Lucas were not a couple, they did have an unspoken understanding between each other. Friends with benefits were what they were. Moreover, nothing more or nothing less, just friends with benefits, but they cared for each other very deeply. Ava knew it was time to move on. Her pride wouldn't allow her to deal with him anymore. She was done and finished with him, even though she loved him. Frank-Lucas had messed his friendship up with Ava over this girl. Ava knew he couldn't love this girl because she felt she had his heart. She felt the connection between them, and she knew he felt it as well. But was this connection real? Or was this connection just in Ava's head? Whether it was or wasn't, Ava was now done with Frank-Lucas and ready to move on with her life.

The same day Ava had seen Frank-Lucas with this girl was the day she was on a date with someone else. Her date was mad about the situation because he wasn't sure why Ava was upset or mad over her ex. Well, he would never understand what she was feeling because he didn't know the connection Ava and Frank-Lucas had. Ava wasn't serious about this guy. He was just passing the time by until she really figured out what she wanted. This was the last time she hung out with this guy. This guy tried seeing her again, but Ava was done and decided to move on. Furthermore, Ava did hear that Frank-Lucas and the girl were done dealing with each other, not by her choice but his. Ava felt good about this because she knew it wasn't going to last. She knew that this girl could never have his heart because she had it. Ava was still angry with Frank-Lucas. She didn't know how to let this situation go, so she still ignored him and kept her distance. Along the way, Ava dated and saw other guys but never got involved in anything serious.

Chapter 6

Ava wanted to forgive Frank-Lucas, and he wanted to talk with her and see her, but she wasn't ready. Ava continued to focus on her life and work. She still avoided seeing Frank-Lucas because she didn't want his eyes or smile to make her forget what he had done. She didn't hate him anymore, but she was still angry and hurt by what he did. Frank-Lucas had a charm that always made Ava forget anything from their past and move forward with their present situation. It was almost like things never happened. Ava was just tired of this repeated cycle of dysfunction. Ava grew up in dysfunction; she didn't want to continue this cycle with Frank-Lucas anymore. It started becoming the norm for them. Ava kept asking God, "Why me?" She prayed to not love Frank-Lucas anymore. She longed for his love and affection, but she couldn't do this anymore.

Partying and having fun on the weekends were on Ava's mind. She just wanted to hang with her friends and forget about Frank-Lucas. Ava danced the night away and had a few drinks. She happened to see Frank-Lucas, but she acted like she didn't. She ignored him and didn't want to talk to him. After the club that night, Ava and some of her friends went to eat at a local Waffle House, and Frank-Lucas came in. He looked good, and that smile was mesmerizing. She hated the way he made her feel. She hated the control he had over her. She still loved Frank-Lucas, and she wanted and desired him. Even after all he had done, she still wanted him. Frank-Lucas worked his normal charm over Ava as he normally did. He apologized for what he did and asked Ava to forgive him. He told her the situation was over and that he missed her. He told her he only wanted her, but she didn't believe him. However, Ava wanted him, whether it was temporary or not, so he went home with her that night. Shaking her head as they talked that night and looking into his eyes, Ava knew it was time for them both to let go. Ava told herself this was going to be the last time she made love to him. She was ready to move forward with her life. She was tired of confusing her heart with a guy who wasn't ready for her. Ava wanted Frank-Lucas to be ready for her, but he wasn't. Ava had plans to move because of a job she got. Ava was so excited to be able to get away from Frank-Lucas. This job was a transfer into another town, away from Frank-Lucas. However, deep down she wanted Frank-Lucas to go with her, but he wasn't ready for that life. So, the two made love, and they both knew this was going to be the last time.

    Ava made some new friends and started seeing the friends she shared with Frank-Lucas. Frank-Lucas was absent from the group, so this was good for Ava. She didn't want to see him anymore. She wanted and needed to be over him. Ava was excited about this new and exciting opportunity at a different bank. This job was full-time and it offered benefits to her. Ava was excited and ready for the change.

One day while out with friends, Ava ran into one of the associates of Frank-Lucas, and he tried to talk to Ava. At first she wasn't interested, but he really kept pursuing her. She finally gave him her number, and they started having conversations thereafter. He knew she had a past with Frank-Lucas, and he told Ava he didn't care. She told him she wasn't looking for anything serious because she wasn't over Frank-Lucas, and she really needed time. He told her everything she didn't want to hear. He even told her some of Frank-Lucas's darkest and deepest secrets that guys normally don't tell girls because of the "man code." She started feeling he didn't really like Frank-Lucas and that he was more into paying Frank-Lucas back for something in their past. He finally told her what it was, so she agreed to sleep with him to pay back Frank-Lucas. Well, they slept together, and it wasn't bad. He really tried to impress Ava. He was great company, and they did have sex multiple times. Ava couldn't get serious with this young man because Frank-Lucas still had her heart. Ava knew it was wrong to do what she did with this guy, but she didn't care at the time. She believed in paying Frank-Lucas back, and she and this guy agreed on that. However, she didn't want Frank-Lucas to find out about this little situation. Ava just wanted to look at him and know that she had slept with someone he knew. Ava just wanted to look in Frank-Lucas's eyes and know she did something that he wouldn't have agreed with. Honestly, Frank-Lucas probably wouldn't have forgiven her if he knew. Maybe this was the thing that Ava wanted Frank-Lucas to find out so they could finally be done, but she wasn't going to tell him. She was going to let this guy or maybe their mutual friends tell him.

Ava was serious about getting over Frank-Lucas. She even pulled herself away from the group and started hanging around other people she had met after her relationship with Frank-Lucas had ended. These friends she had met them in the town she worked. They were nice and loved to party. Ava was down for that because she enjoyed partying as well. Things for Ava was finally coming together. She was finally seeing away up from being so down from walking away from Frank-Lucas.

Chapter 7

Ava started going out with a group of friends she had met through a friend she worked with at her new job. She was familiar with two of the people. Moreover, she even remembered one of the roommates because he would stop by the store she worked at. Furthermore, she went to school with this guy's stepson. The guy mentioned he was newly divorced. This guy was much older than Ava, so she wasn't interested. He tried pursuing her before at her job, but she shut him down very nicely. Ava was OK with being friends with the roommates and hanging out, but Ava wasn't into any of the guys there at the party. That night they had a drink or two, and she didn't remember much thereafter. Ava wasn't a big drinker, but that night everything went blank. Ava woke up in the bed with this older guy. Ava felt very uncomfortable because she couldn't remember anything after the second drink she'd had. This was very unusual for Ava because she never would stay somewhere she was not completely sure of. Ava jumped out the bed scared, and she grabbed her keys and left. Ava left her shoes and jacket at this guy's house. She couldn't remember anything, especially consenting to sex. She didn't feel right, and the only other guy she had been with previously without protection was Frank-Lucas.

This was so hard for Ava. She wasn't able to tell any of her friends because she was prideful and ashamed. Ava was off work that Sunday morning, so she stayed in that whole day. Ava went to the doctor that Monday morning to have herself checked out. Her doctor advised her to take the morning after pill. This was terrifying for Ava. She never really had to deal with anything of this situation before. Ava had to have STD test multiple times within a few months. Ava didn't tell anyone about this situation. She cried herself to sleep at night thinking about it. Luckily all of Ava's test came back clean. She was angry at herself because she wondered how this could have happened to her. She was smart and very intuitive. Ava should have known something wasn't right.

During this time, Ava longed to talk with Frank-Lucas. All she wanted was him. She wanted to hug him, feel his touch, and talk to him, but she couldn't. Part of the reason for her going to that party was to try and not think about Frank-Lucas, but all she wanted was him. As much as she wanted to move on from Frank-Lucas, there was just always something that felt quite familiar to her with him. She really did love him, and she really had a soulful connection with him. It was like he was intuitive of her feelings. He always knew the right time to come around.

Ava received great news from the doctor. She was clear of all diseases. Ava gave praises to God and told him she would do better, and she did. Ava decided to cut back the drinking and partying. She also only hung out with people she trusted. Moreover, Ava made

Frank-Lucas use protection the few times thereafter that they had sex. She didn't trust anyone at that time. She was disease free, and Frank-Lucas had slept with a girl she knew, she wasn't going to sleep behind that girl without protection.

The continued cycle of Ava and Frank-Lucas happened a few more times but with protection. Ava so desired Frank-Lucas to want her the way she wanted him. He loved Ava, and Ava somehow knew this; it just wasn't enough for him to get himself together. Frank-Lucas was out there. He was living a carefree life and dibbling and dabbling into drugs and all sorts of things. Ava knew this life. She had seen her dad do these same things. Moreover, in a way, Frank-Lucas reminded Ava of her dad in some ways. Ava had always desired a relationship with her dad. Ava knew her dad loved her, but she believed he loved the streets more and drugs more. Just as Frank-Lucas was emotionally unavailable to her at times, this was the same with her dad. Ava loved her dad and she loved Frank-Lucas but she knew they were incapable of showing their emotions. Ava needed and desired this from them both. Ava forgave Frank-Lucas and really wanted to keep a friendship with him, but she was moving on from him. Ava wanted to date, but she was scared. She wanted and desired to settle down. She wished it could have been with Frank-Lucas, but again, he wasn't ready for that. So Ava slept with Frank-Lucas for the last time. She knew that night would be the last time they would lie in her bed together. Ava watched him while he slept. She listened to his breathing and watched his chest rise up and down. Ava loved Frank-Lucas dearly. She was in love with this young man, but she knew it wasn't their time.

Chapter 8

Ava started putting away her thoughts of what happened that night in the fall. Ava also started putting Frank-Lucas behind her. She was starting to finally see the light and imagine life without Frank-Lucas. Ava was ready for something fresh and new. Besides, her mother told her a year ago, "In order to get over one man, you have to get under a new one." She was playing, but Ava thought it might be a good idea. Well, Ava learned that wasn't true, but she moved on anyway. While at work, Ava met a young man who came by her job quite often to see her. He admired Ava, and Ava found him interesting and cute. This guy was amazing. He was the kind of guy you would want to bring home to meet your parents. Jack was shy and polite. He was very much interested in Ava but too scared to ask for her number. Jack's roommate asked Ava for her number, and she gave it to him. Jack was so disappointed that his roommate asked for Ava's number first. Ava wasn't interested in the roommate. She was curious to get to know Jack. Jack was different from the guys she dated in the past. Jack was totally different from Frank-Lucas but different was what she wanted and needed.

One night, Ava got a phone call, and it was from Jack. Immediately, Ava knew who was on the phone. Jack's voice was shaky, and she could tell he was nervous. Ava was excited to get the phone call from Jack. That night Jack and Ava talked all night long. They got very familiar with each other. Both had to be at work the next morning. These two had so many things in common. Ava liked that he was hardworking and a family man. She liked that they had so much in common with each other. It was almost like she was seeing herself in him. Ava thought she had finally found someone to make her forget about Frank-Lucas. She was at ease and felt there was finally hope for her when it came to finding someone she was compatible with. Over a few weeks, Ava and Jack started getting to know each other. Ava found out her and Jack had the same exact birthday. She couldn't believe this, and neither could he. Jack would come to Ava's job to see her multiple times a week. The two started getting really friendly with each other. Ava really liked the friendship these two began to have with each other.

In addition, Ava mentioned to Jack that she was coming out of a complicated situation. He asked her if this was with her ex. He assumed it was with her child's father. She explained that it wasn't her child's dad but someone else she was seeing. She let him know she still had feelings for this person. Ava wanted to be as honest as possible with Jack. Jack didn't care because he really liked Ava, and he knew he could make her forget Frank-Lucas. Jack even reassured her of this. Ava was happy at that moment. She wanted to be free from the hold Frank-Lucas had over her. Jack was one of the good guys. He was everything Ava was looking for. He wasn't perfect, but he was a good person, and he adored Ava. Jack knew he could be the man Ava needed. He was confident in himself. Jack told Ava he had been with many women before her, but he hadn't met one like her. He found Ava interesting. She was independent and confident in herself. He liked this about her. Jack liked that Ava had herself together. He loved her smile and her beauty. Ava was everything that Jack was looking for; however, Jack was in a little situation that Ava knew nothing about. It ended quickly, and he told Ava about it because she told him she had no time for nonsense. He reassured Ava that the situation was over and that it wasn't anything serious. Ava believed him, and they continued to be friends.

Jack started falling for Ava quickly. Ava cared for Jack as well, but she wanted to remain friends. She didn't want to make the mistake of moving too quickly. What she had with Jack was so different than what she had with Frank-Lucas. She fell very quickly for Frank-Lucas. The connection she had with Frank-Lucas was out of this world and nothing she had never experienced. But Jack was the right man. She didn't want her past to mess up what she presently had with Jack. Ava wasn't where Jack was in their relationship, but she really liked him. Ava could see her life with Jack.

These two became really great friends. Their relationship became more serious. Jack even got alone with Ava's son, even though the five-year-old gave him a hard time. Jack wasn't easy to scare off. Jack was exactly a year younger than Ava, but one would have thought he was much older because of his maturity. Jack wanted something real with Ava, and Ava wanted something real with him as well. However, she wasn't over Frank-Lucas yet. Ava tried forgetting Frank-Lucas. She wanted to be over Frank-Lucas, but she just couldn't shake the feeling of loving him.

Time passed, and every day got better. Ava really started forgetting Frank-Lucas. She felt if he was out of sight, then she could get over him. Ava ran into Frank-Lucas one night after the club, and it was so hard for her to see him. Everything she once felt for him came back to her immediately. She wasn't going to sleep with him, but she wanted to talk with him. Ava called Frank-Lucas that next morning because she wanted him to let go of her completely, so she could finally move on with her life. Jack was serious about being with Ava. He saw them as a family. He asked Ava to marry him, and Ava said yes. She just had to have the talk with Frank-Lucas. She wanted Frank-Lucas to free her. Ava wanted to free Frank-Lucas. She knew the two had such a strong connection, but she knew it was time for them to let go.

Ava saw Frank-Lucas that morning, and it was so hard for her to be in his presence. She knew this would probably be the last time she would see him. Ava never told him she had moved on and was planning to marry someone else, but seeing Frank-Lucas for the last time would hopefully give Ava the closure she needed from him.

Chapter 9

Ava and Jack finally got married. Ava didn't think they were completely ready, but the two couldn't see life without each other. Ava and Jack moved together and formed their already made family. Ava met some of Jack's family, and Jack met her family as well. Their family thought they were crazy for getting married at such a young age and not dating longer. Ava felt safe with Jack. The two had such a strong compatibility with each other. They both were hardworking and very ambitious. Ava didn't have the connection with Jack that she had with Frank-Lucas. Ava didn't have the sexual chemistry with Jack that she had with Frank-Lucas. But Ava adored Jack. She loved how he loved her and how he showed her and her son love. These two got alone and became like best friends. Their relationship was a pure friendship. Ava wished that she had waited before marrying so soon, but she didn't want to risk losing someone great like Jack. Deep inside, Ava still loved Frank-Lucas, but she wanted things to work between her and Jack. Jack was such an amazing man.

But as great as Jack was, he wasn't Frank-Lucas. Ava tried making love to Jack, but it was hard at first because all she could think about was Frank-Lucas. This wasn't fair to Jack. Jack did feel this deep down. He constantly asked her what was wrong. She would tell him nothing, but deep down she knew what it was. Ava cried many nights because she missed Frank-Lucas. She cared for Jack so much, but she was still in love with Frank-Lucas.

Jack wouldn't give up on Ava. She was worth the wait. He knew he could make her forget Frank-Lucas. He just thought they needed time. Things did get better with the two. The relationship grew stronger. These two were best friends, and they cared deeply for one another. They had love for each other on another level, and they worked well together. These two started gaining so much together in their marriage. However, things weren't perfect, but what relationship was? Jack had a habit of conversating with other women over emails and texts. Even though Ava had love for Frank-Lucas, she never acted on it. Ava tried respecting the union her and Jack created. She wanted to be a good wife. She tried doing everything right. The only thing that was missing was the love Jack felt he needed from Ava.

Ava did love Jack; it just wasn't in the way he loved her. Jack had this feeling inside about his wife that made him feel the need to get comfort through conversation from other women. Jack needed the attention he lacked from Ava. Ava wanted to give him the attention he so desired but she couldn't. She couldn't love him the way he desired her to. Jack said he never had a sexual relationship with these other women, but he did have emotional conversations about his wife that really hurt Ava. Ava tried to get over the issues that she had with Jack. This really bothered Ava, and she felt alone within their marriage. Ava knew deep down that she cared deeply for Jack, and she wanted to make the marriage work. Ava didn't want to feel like a failure. Ava forgave Jack, and they tried moving on from these situations.

Chapter 10

Ava and Jack moved out of the town they were staying in. This was farther from the situations with these women. These two moved on with their lives. Things weren't perfect, but they were OK. They both worked really hard and started achieving more within the marriage. There was a lot going against the marriage. Jack was back to his old ways, and Ava was fed up. She wanted him to feel the way she felt. She wanted him to hurt like her. Ava decided to go out with some of her friends one night back in her hometown. Ava happened to run into Frank-Lucas that night. This was some years after the two got married. She was tired of being a good wife. Ava would have never cheated on Jack with just anybody, but Frank-Lucas felt familiar to her. Ava and Frank-Lucas always had a repeated cycle of coming back to each other. The two looked into each other's eyes, and immediately it was love at first sight again. The two confessed their love for one another, and it felt nice. However, there was one thing different about this time: Ava was married! Ava had a deep conversation with Frank-Lucas, and Frank-Lucas asked her why she had gotten married. Ava told him it was because she wanted to move on from him and that Jack was a good man. She told Frank-Lucas she has always had love in her heart for him, but she let him know she couldn't and wouldn't wait for him.

Frank-Lucas had tears in his eyes because deep down he knew Ava was the one and only true love for him, but he still wasn't ready for her. Ava and Frank-Lucas spent the night together at a hotel. Ava knew it was wrong, but she still loved this man. She started feeling guilty immediately because as imperfect as Jack was, Ava knew he didn't deserve what she had done to him. Ava felt bad and wanted to tell him, but she still had feelings for Frank-Lucas. However, Ava knew Frank-Lucas was still the same. She knew Frank-Lucas wasn't ready for her once again, so she made her mind up to walk away from Frank-Lucas. This situation was once again very hard for Ava, but she had to do it.

Ava decided to tell Jack what she had done. Jack was furious with Ava, but he loved her and wanted things to work. Jack didn't ask too many questions about the situation because he knew he had made a few mistakes. Jack knew he could eventually forgive Ava because he wanted it to work with her. Ava was the one that he wanted to spend the rest of his life with. It took some time, but Jack forgave Ava, and they moved forward with their lives. Ava lost all contact with Frank-Lucas, and she finally felt like she was free from him. Every day got better and better. Ava even decided to lean back from the mutual friends they shared so that she couldn't and wouldn't have to hear about him. Ava and Jack were in a good place with their marriage. They even decided they were going to try and have a baby.

There were a few hiccups during this new chapter in Ava and Jack's life. Every time they got a stumbling block, they seemed to get over it; however, one of the hardest ones was when Jack's mom came to live with them for a while. This was such a hard time for Jack and Ava because Jack was the baby of his family. He loved his mother, but she almost seemed jealous of Ava and Jack's relationship. Moreover, Jack's mother criticized everything in Jack and Ava's home. Jack and Ava really tried everything. Jack's mother roasted Ava because Ava didn't iron Jack's clothes. She made Ava feel really small in her own home. Ava knew Jack's mom didn't want to be there with them because she said it before coming. Jack's mom had already helped ruined Jack's sister's marriage; now she was working on Jack and Ava's marriage to. Things got so bad that Ava had her mind made up to walk away from the marriage; however, she wasn't walking away from the home she and Jack had bought.

Ava was fed up with Jack's mom. She was ready for her to leave. One night things got so bad that Ava screamed, started throwing things around, and called out Jack's mom's name. She was done and demanded for her to get out of her home. Ava couldn't take any more of Jack's mom, so Jack drove her back to his sister's house.

Things weren't right with Ava and Jack for a while. Even though they loved each other, they both were mad at each other. Ava was angry with Jack because she felt he let his mom come into their home and ruin their marriage. Ava felt Jack never put his mom in her place. She felt that he acted like a little kid when his mom was around. Ava didn't want to be married to a little boy. She needed a man who would have her back. Jack didn't do this or be the person she needed him to be. Furthermore, Jack was angry with Ava because Ava had called his mom a "BITCH". Ava did apologize for what she said to his mother, but his mom told Jack's siblings, and they hated Ava. They wanted Jack to leave Ava.

Ava was so over this relationship and Jack's family. The only person who talked to Ava was Jack's dad, who was residing in another Country. Jack's mom kept things going within the family. The family enabled Jack's mother's behavior and didn't see any wrong, but to Ava, she was evil. Ava could see right through her. Ava was ready to walk away, but deep down, she did love Jack and really couldn't see life without him. Ava had grown to love Jack deeply, but she was ready to walk away. Things grew so complicated with Ava and Jack that they started sleeping in separate rooms.

Chapter 11

Ava and Jack got through the situation with his mom. They decided to work on their marriage. The two of them decided to go through counseling and work through their problems. Ava did not have a relationship with Jack's family. Jack only had a relationship with Ava's family. Things were once again becoming rocky between the two. They wanted to have a baby—or Ava wanted to give Jack a baby because this was his heart's desire. He had no biological kids of his own, but he had helped Ava raise her son since he was five. Ava didn't want any more kids, but she knew this was what Jack wanted. The two tried and tried to get pregnant, but it didn't happen right away. The two of them had to go through fertility treatment. This was really tough for them, especially Ava. She had to do injections, and they had to time sex. It was tough for these two. The marriage and relationship were being tested once again.

After about six months, Ava and Jack finally conceived their son. This was a blessing for them. This brought the two of them together even closer. They were finally in a really great place in their marriage. Moreover, the marriage and pregnancy were going great, until Jack had a slipup. Jack went back to some of his old ways. He was still having conversations with a lady he worked with. He was hiding this from Ava. Ava thought the marriage was going great. Ava had no clue what Jack was doing. She was finally happy and in a good place with Jack—at least, she thought she was. Ava and Jack's family was finally in a great place. They were talking, and things were going well. Furthermore, the family came to visit for the baby shower. Things were going great until Ava happened to find an email from a lady that Jack was talking with. The conversation got really deep between these two. Ava was heartbroken. She thought things were finally good with her and Jack. Ava started stressing out and became very angry with Jack. She was over this relationship and was ready to walk away once again.

Jack begged Ava to not leave him. He cried and wanted his family together. He wanted Ava to forgive him so they could move forward. Ava couldn't really trust Jack, but she tried. However, it was hard for her. Ava and Jack went forward with their marriage and worked things out for the sake of their kid. Ava and Jack had a healthy baby, and life went on for them. Life wasn't bad, and Ava and Jack were doing really great. Ava didn't forget about what Jack had done, but she was willing to forgive him and try and move forward. Things continued to be OK between the two—until they hit another roadblock.

At this time Ava's brother and wife moved in with them. It tested their marriage and household. The two got through this, but then Ava's dad got sick and had to move in with them. The marriage was being tested again, and these two were going through things because of family. Ava's dad passed, and the two decided that they weren't going to let anyone else move in again. Ava's brother and family moved out as well. Ava and Jack were getting on track finally—and then Jack did it again. Jack started another emotional afair. Jack swore it was only talk but Ava didn't really know if he was telling the truth.

Jack hurt Ava this time to the core. Ava knew things wouldn't be the same between the two. Ava had lost so much trust with Jack, and their relationship was tried again. She wanted to pay Jack back, but she wouldn't just pay him back with just anybody. Ava lived her life and hung out with her girlfriends. Ava had many times to get Jack back, but she wasn't going to do it with just anybody. Ava continued to be angry with Jack because she felt like he messed their family up. Ava couldn't get past it this time. Ava just went with the flow of things, but she had checked out of the marriage.

Ava was living life and trying to function through her pain and frustrations with Jack. To make things even worse, one of her mutual friends of Frank-Lucas mentioned he had gotten married. Deep down Ava was happy for him but the other side was sad because it wasn't her. Ava was already married but unhappy in that marriage. She wanted to be happy for Frank-Lucas but she was a little envy of this lady, she knew nothing about. Ava couldn't believe this lady got Frank-Lucas to settle down. In addition, to marrying someone, she found out Frank-Lucas had two more kids years earlier by two different women. Ava thought to herself what a mess his wife would have to deal with. She thought better her than me. Ava was a little selfish because she still cared for Frank-Lucas and always thought one day they would be together. At least in her mind. Ava knew it wasn't meant for her and Frank-Lucas to be together, it just was never their time.

Chapter 12

Ava and Jack kept the family together. Things weren't great, but they functioned. Ava and Jack never dealt with the situation of the emotional affairs that Jack had with these women. The last two emotional affairs Jack had were with the same women. Ava was done inside. She couldn't look at Jack the same anymore. Also, Ava's brother moved in with Jack and Ava until his place became available. After he moved out, Jack's dad moved in for a few years. Things just got worse for these two. Ava wanted to have her family to herself for sometime. During the course of Ava's and Jack's marriage, they've always had someone there. How could a marriage be solid when someone is always in the middle of it? This was the case for these two. They really never had the time to really become one because they've always had family involved in the marriage and living with them.

Ava and Jack got a surprise. They found out that Ava was pregnant. Ava was almost six months pregnant when they found out.

Ava worked long nights at the local hospital and never had a sign of pregnancy. She was dealing with fatige but who wasn't during Covid-19 in 2020. Ava was overworked didn't notice any changes in her body. Ava didn't have a menstrual because of her PCOS. This was very common for her. Moreover, Ava was taken birth control prior to getting pregnant and this helped regulate her menstrual. Ava stopped the birth control in May of 2020 due to a bloodclot in her right leg. This had to be the time she conceived the baby. This was surprising to Ava because her fertility doctor told her that she would never conceive another child unless she repeated fertility again.

This child was a blessing but the timing was off for Ava and Jack because their marriage wasn't in a great place. Ava was ready to leave Jack. Jack thought she was dealing with hormones, which she was, but she wasn't happy. Ava wanted to clear the house out, and she wanted to move forward from the relationship. Jack didn't want this, and he didn't make things easier. Jack might have thought Ava was complaining as she does sometimes, but this time it was more than that. Ava felt she needed to find herself and reconnect with the person inside. She was so used to taking care of everyone else that she neglected herself at times.

Ava gave birth to a healthy little girl. This was a happy moment for the two; however, it didn't make the marriage better, but it brought a bit of joy in the home. Things went on, and these two functioned through life as if there were no problems. Ava decided she wasn't having more kids, and she wanted to lose weight and work on herself. Ava achieved this and felt really good. Ava achieved great health, and she felt good about herself. Jack enjoyed what he saw as well, and he liked the new Ava. Jack even thought

Ava's self-esteem had improved. Ava didn't notice it, but she knew she felt great. Ava was finally starting to feel happy with herself. She was done having kids and wanted to start putting herself and needs first for the first time in a long time. Ava really wanted to reinvent herself. She started thinking of creative ideas that she could put into play. Ava loved to write; it was just that she never had much time to do it.

Chapter 13

Ava was home one day doing her normal weekly routine. Ava got a text message from her brother and a friend. The news wasn't great. They told her that Frank-Lucas's mother had passed away. This was devastating news because Ava knew how close Frank-Lucas was with his mom. Frank-Lucas was the baby of his family and his mother's only boy. He loved her, and she loved him. The two of them were like best friends. Ava didn't have a relationship with Frank-Lucas's mother, but they had met many years ago. Ava and her friends decided to get together to go and pay their respects in regard to the passing of Frank-Lucas's mother. Ava and her friends arrived, and there was no sign of Frank-Lucas. It was almost a relief because Ava and Frank-Lucas hadn't seen each other in many years. Moreover, Ava was still married, and she heard Frank-Lucas was married with two more kids. Ava and her friends decided to write their names in the book of visitors so Frank-Lucas would know that they were there.

Deep down Ava wanted to see him, but she knew it might be a bad idea; besides, he was married and so was she. Moreover, Ava always told herself that Frank-Lucas was better off remaining in her heart than in her life. This was the story she kept telling herself throughout the years. Ava and her friends ran into one of his kids mother. The one that gave Ava such a hard time. They talked to her and the conversation was grownup. Ava had no hard feeling against this girl anymore. She wasn't planning to be friends with her but she could be cordial. Ava's friend on the other end didn't forgive so easily, lets just say, she still didn't like her.

As Ava and her friends started to walk away from the funeral home, Frank-Lucas pulled up. It had been such a long time since they had seen each other, and she didn't know how it would feel seeing him. Well, Frank-Lucas came up to the friends and hugged them. At first he didn't recognize Ava because it had been so long since they'd seen each other, and Ava had lost a little weight since the last time they saw each other. Frank-Lucas called her name out and immediately told her he loved her. Ava was shocked to hear that from him. Ava even told him to be quiet because he was married, and his wife might be there. He told Ava he had separated from his wife and that they were no longer together. Moreover, he looked around to see if she was by herself, and she confirmed she was. Ava and Frank-Lucas hadn't seen each other in so long, but they wanted to catch up. Immediately, there was such a connection between the two. Frank-Lucas asked Ava if he could have a hug, and she agreed. It felt very familiar to Ava and Frank-Lucas because they always had a physical and emotional connection. Ava had missed Frank-Lucas, and by the look and sound of things, Frank-Lucas had missed Ava too.

In addition, these two always had chemistry and love for one another. It always seemed organic and pure. It was hard for these two to be around each other because of their past. Ava always felt safer staying at a distance since they'd had that encounter over thirteen years ago. Ava knew that Frank-Lucas still had some feelings for her because a mutual friend would mention it every once in a while. Ava would brush it off because she thought Frank-Lucas was still the same young man she knew many years ago. She didn't believe him, but deep down inside she could feel him in her heart. These two had such a connection that Ava could almost feel when Frank-Lucas was in pain. It was hard for her to explain this to anyone, so she kept it to herself. She knew it sounded crazy, and she could never understand what it was about Frank-Lucas. She assumed he was somehow her twin flame or soulmate.

Now Ava had grown to love Jack. Their love was different from what she had shared with Frank-Lucas. Ava and Frank-Lucas had an instant connection. When Ava met Frank-Lucas, it was almost like she had known him in a past life. It felt magical and organic. However, it had moved really quickly with the two of them twenty-one years earlier. Ava had always loved Frank-Lucas, but she knew he wouldn't change his ways back then. Ava refused to wait on him. She wanted to live her life and try to find some happiness outside him.

Continuing on, Ava was about to leave with her friends, and Frank-Lucas asked her to put his number in her phone. Ava hesitated because she knew it wasn't a good idea. However, instead of listening to her inner voice, Ava listened to her heart. She felt at home with Frank-Lucas. It felt so familiar and warm with him. She was stepping into a territory that wasn't good. Nothing about the situation was right, but it just felt so good at the moment. So Ava received his number. He told her she could put it in her phone as someone else; Ava did it. She knew it wasn't a good idea, but she and Jack weren't in a good solid place. Ava wanted to catch up with Frank-Lucas. She wanted to know how life had been for him and what he had been up to.

Ava waited three days before reaching out to Frank-Lucas. She typed him a text and then deleted the message more than five times. She was scared to reach out to him. It didn't feel right, but she was curious. Ava finally sent the text. Frank-Lucas reached back out to her immediately. Ava had butterflies in her stomach. It felt amazing to be communicating with Frank-Lucas. Moreover, she wanted to be friends with him because she missed him. Ava still had feelings for Frank-Lucas, and she cared about his well-being.

As the two continued to text each other, they started learning things about each other that they didn't know. It wasn't enough that they were texting each other, but the texts became phone calls. Ava always initiated the texts and calls because Frank-Lucas wanted to try and be respectful of Ava's marriage and family. Ava knew that Jack would never see this situation as good. However, Ava was so caught up in the moments of talking with Frank-Lucas that she forgot about her family. She functioned and did her normal routine, but she was even happier because she had something exciting going on in her life. Besides, things were just so boring and "the norm" with Jack. Jack seemed checked out of the marriage. Things just felt good with Frank-Lucas. The two of them started enjoying each other's conversations. Things started to get really personal and very heated. Ava and Frank-Lucas both started confessing their love for each other—and then that was it. They both agreed that they were both scared and not ready for each other during the time they met years ago. However, the two knew back then that they wanted to be together, but Ava wasn't going to tell Frank-Lucas how she felt, and he didn't tell her either. The two of them felt angry with each other because they had never really told each other how they really felt.

Ava and Frank-Lucas were planning to see each other. Ava was scared to be around Frank-Lucas because she didn't know what would happen. She knew she had such a strong connection to him and a physical attraction. She loved him and always kept him in her heart. Ava was finally able to tell him how she really felt. She was ready to see him. She wanted to lay eyes on him and see what his life was like. She spoke with him on a daily basis, and they planned to see each other.

Chapter 14

Ava and Frank-Lucas decided to see each other. It had been almost a month since they reconnected. They spoke every day for almost a month through texts, videos, and phone calls. Ava and Frank-Lucas wanted to see each other so badly. That day was nerve-racking for Ava. It had been so long since she and Frank-Lucas were together. They had been talking and confessing their love for one another for this past month, and they both were ready to see one another. Ava arrived to see Frank-Lucas, and he was sitting on the porch talking with one of his neighbors. Ava got out of her vehicle to walk up to the porch, and Frank-Lucas's neighbor said Ava was fine. Frank-Lucas mentioned to him that Ava was all right. Ava knew she looked good. Frank-Lucas tried putting on his uninterested face, but deep down she knew he wanted her. This didn't bother Ava because she knew how Frank-Lucas was. Frank-Lucas has always tried to down-play his feelings. He wanted to look hard but Ava could read right through him. Ava went in and had a seat. Frank-Lucas followed thereafter. The two started a conversation, and then they went up to Frank-Lucas's room. Ava was a little shy. She hadn't been with Frank-Lucas in thirteen years, and during that time it was quick and more meaningless. Ava had such a strong attraction to Frank-Lucas. Ava's body felt unreal being next to him. Ava was very sexually attracted to Frank-Lucas. She wanted him, and he wanted her.

The two used protection and did this one more time thereafter. Sex wasn't the greatest with Frank-Lucas, but for whatever reason, Ava was sexually attracted to him. Her body yearned for his touch. Frank-Lucas wasn't romantic or anything, but she just loved him for him. Ava didn't know why he made her feel the way she felt. She knew it was wrong, but she just couldn't help herself. She desired Frank-Lucas in her life, and she was determined to keep him there, no matter the cost.

Frank-Lucas and Ava were debating how to make this love affair or love triangle work. Ava didn't want to lose her family, but she didn't want to let go of Frank-Lucas either. So the two of them decided they would be girlfriend and boyfriend. Ava would remain married and the wife that Jack needed her to be. She didn't want to lose her family, but she didn't want to give up Frank-Lucas, either, so they made the relationship work. Moreover, Ava didn't want Frank-Lucas to see any other women while they were together. Ava knew this was selfish of her, but she wanted Frank-Lucas all to herself; she didn't want to share him. Frank-Lucas agreed to this arrangement. This love triangle reminded Ava of her younger days with Cole and Luke. Yeah, she was selfish but Ava felt she had enough love to go around, at least with two men.

Ava agreed to try and see him once a week. Ava helped with meals and groceries when she was there. It didn't become about sex anymore because the two had something much deeper. Ava loved Frank-Lucas for who he was. She didn't care about the sex; she just wanted to be in his life. Furthermore, it got harder and harder for Ava to leave him each week. Ava starting feeling like something was missing. She felt lonely being at home with Jack. Jack really didn't pay much attention to Ava until he wanted to have sex, but then one day out of the blue, Jack started changing. It seemed Jack knew Ava was pulling away from him. She was on her phone more and smiled even more.

Chapter 15

Jack knew something wasn't right with Ava. He was trying to do the things that Ava wanted him to do for the last eighteen years. At this point it was too late for her and Jack. Ava had stepped out on the marriage. She was done in her mind. Ava didn't want to try anymore. She loved Jack, but she felt she couldn't give him more. Ava just wanted the kids to be OK. She knew if Jack found out about her and Frank-Lucas that things would probably be over. A few times during her visits with Frank-Lucas, Ava wanted to break things off with him. Ava's conscience bothered her quite a bit. She knew going to see Frank-Lucas was wrong, but she almost felt obligated. She wanted to be there for him. She knew how it felt to lose someone you love, especially your mother. She needed to be there for Frank-Lucas. She didn't want to hurt Jack or Frank-Lucas, but Ava was confused. She realized that she wanted to make her family work, but she also wanted to keep Frank-Lucas in her life.

Ava had gone back to work, and Jack was starting to snoop through Ava's things. He wanted to see what she was up to and whom she was talking to. So Jack put a recording device in Ava's work bag. Moreover, he followed her one morning when she lied to him and said she was going to work. Well, she didn't; she went to Frank-Lucas house. Ava had probably been there fifteen minutes, and then Jack showed up. Jack had followed her to Frank-Lucas's house. Jack came to the door and asked for his wife. He was angry with Ava. He had already pulled up Frank-Lucas's information. Well, at least he thought he did. He had the wrong person online. It wasn't the same person. In Jack's mind, he thought Ava was seeing different guys, but this wasn't true. Jack just had the wrong guy. Jack found a man by the same name as Frank-Lucas and thought this was the person. When he came to Frank-Lucas door he seen someone he wasn't expecting. Jack had already called this other guys wife and left a message for her letting her know things were about to go down. He had the wrong Frank-lucas on paper and the wrong wife.

Ava went outside to try and calm Jack down. Jack was so angry with Ava. He called her many names out of anger and hurt. He even told her he was getting a DNA test for the kids. Honestly, at the moment, Ava deserved it. Jack was hurt; Ava had broken his heart. He couldn't take seeing Ava with another man. Jack had told Ava to come home and get her things and get out. He had disappointment in his eyes toward her. He mentioned to her that she was his best friend and he asked her how she could hurt him this way. Jack had every message that Frank-Lucas and Ava had ever written to one another since September. Jack left with his friend, and Ava went back in the house to get her bag. She found out Jack had been recording her and checking through their phone records. Jack had done things like this before. Ava had nothing to hide up until September. Ava really never trusted Jack anymore after his last situation with the lady who worked for the same company he did. Ava knew the relationship was over. She knew Jack wouldn't forgive her. Jack was angry with her, and he had said some very hurtful things to Ava. Ava deserved some of what he said, but Ava wasn't this person. She wasn't a whore, or this person Jack described her as being.

Ava arrived home, and she and Jack discussed what was next for them. Jack was still processing his anger and feelings. He was so hurt and angry with Ava. Ava apologized to Jack. She told him she was sorry and that she never really wanted to purposely hurt him. She also mentioned she loved him but loved Frank-Lucas as well. Ava was so confused. She did love both of these guys. She didn't want to hurt either of them, but Ava really needed time to process her feelings and emotions. She loved the life she and Jack had built, but she couldn't just let go of Frank-Lucas either. He felt a part of her. Ava felt like Frank-Lucas had a purpose in her life; she just didn't know what it was.

Days had passed, and Ava and Frank-Lucas had no contact. Ava messaged a friend for them to get a message to Frank-Lucas. She knew Jack was tracking her phone but she didn't care anymore. She wanted Frank-Lucas to know she was OK. She felt bad about how everything went down. She never wanted Jack to show up at Frank-Lucas's house. She was embarrassed and angry at the same time. Ava and Jack both talked to each other every day. They cried together, argued, and tried talking over things and discussing how things had gotten to this point. Jack seemed as if he wanted to forgive Ava and move on, but Ava was done with the marriage. She never really trusted Jack after his last situation. She was done before they found out they were having their last child. Ava tried to forgive Jack and move on, but it was hard. Ava knew the marriage was over between her and Jack. She knew this was what was going to make her and Jack move forward with their lives.

By this time the New Year had come around, and Ava and Jack were both still in the same situation as last year. They both decided they would separate but couldn't afford to separate into different living situations. Ava started working more, and Jack started helping more around the house and with the kids. Ava still kept in touch with Frank-Lucas, but she had to break up with him because she really didn't know what she wanted at the time. However, she knew she cared for him, but she knew she wasn't ready for a relationship with him. Moreover, he wasn't really ready for her either. Frank-Lucas had some scars and situations in his life he needed to work on. Ava saw this with Frank-Lucas. He had trust issues, and he was trying to recover and work on himself. Ava and Frank-Lucas knew they were better off as friends, so that is what they remained.

Ava and Jack had bittersweet moments. When it came to finances, this was an argument every time for them. Moreover, when it came to them agreeing where they should reside after the divorce was even a bigger issue for them. Jack made more money than Ava, and Ava was still in school trying to finish up. She really couldn't afford to go live anywhere else on her budget. Ava was lonely again at home, not being able to see Frank-Lucas. She missed their conversations because they didn't talk as much as they once did due to Jack and all his investigations. Ava didn't want to live like a prisoner anymore. She wanted to be free. She wanted to be financially free from Jack, and she wanted to be able to take care of herself. She knew it was going to be hard being a single mother again, but she knew she could do it. It would take some hard work and dedication, but she could do it. Besides, Jack was a great dad. He loved his kids and wanted to be a father.

Chapter 16

Ava carried on with life. She managed coparenting with Jack and working full time. Frank-Lucas and Ava remained in contact with each other. They talked less and less often. Ava felt as if Frank-Lucas had no reason to prove himself to her anymore. Ava believed he felt he had her exactly where he wanted her. Ava still felt some confusion when it came to her and Frank-Lucas. She noticed he was hot and cold with her. She noticed Frank-Lucas got comfortable, as if Ava wouldn't leave him because he knew she loved him. Frank-Lucas was spoiled and very self-absorbed. Ava started thinking she didn't have time to raise another kid; besides she had two young kids of her own.

The more Ava and Frank-Lucas talked and really got to know the people they were, the more she started to lose interest in Frank-Lucas. Ava tested Frank-Lucas to see if he really was serious about pursuing a relationship with her. She tested him in so many ways, and with the entire test, Frank-Lucas failed miserably. Ava knew that it was time to let go of what she and Frank-Lucas shared. That soul tie was not working for Ava anymore. Their friendship started becoming more and more toxic. Ava thought to herself that is this the man I really want to spend my life with? She was ready to be free from her entangled, sultry love affair with Frank-Lucas. Ava wanted to see where things could go with her and Frank-Lucas, but Frank-Lucas wasn't ready to be what Ava wanted and needed. He was a man-child. Frank-Lucas wanted to have Ava but not the responsibilities that came with being someone's boyfriend.

Ava asked Frank-Lucas why he was pulling away from her, and he replied, "he wasn't pulling away. Ava knew something wasn't right with him. She couldn't pinpoint it but she knew things were off with the two of them. So, one night, Ava and Jack was having a conversation, and Jack told Ava that he called Frank-Lucas and had a man to man conversation. Ava was in shock. Jack went on to say that he asked Frank-Lucas to back off from Ava. He told Frank-Lucas Ava was confused and didn't know exactly what she wanted. This may have been the case earlier on in their love triangle but those feelings started to change. Ava was so mad at Jack. It bothered her that Jack would go behind her back and do that. It felt like control all over again. Ava was fed up with him in this moment. She really wanted to be done with her and Jack's relationship.

Things started to get real with Frank-Lucas at this time. He was coming out of what was comfortable for him. He had been separated from his wife for two years, and he enjoyed his freedom. He enjoyed seeing Ava sometimes and getting all the benefits of a boyfriend and girlfriend situation but not having to provide anything full time. Ava didn't want anything too serious yet, but she wanted Frank-Lucas to be better for himself and maybe one day for her. Ava was willing to wait for him to get it together. She just needed him to show interest in what she desired and needed for her life, but Frank-Lucas was too selfish to even see beyond himself and his own needs.

Ava woke up one day and decided it was time to move on with her life. She wanted to see what was out there so she could know that there is life beyond Frank-Lucas. Ava went on a date, a double date. She had a really great time, and the guy was very attractive and nice. He had such a great personality. This guy had been divorced for a few years, and he had two adolescent children. They both seemed to hit it off, but Ava didn't want to get too serious with this guy before talking with Frank-Lucas and seeing where his head was. She liked him a little. She knew she could move forward with her life and away from Frank-Lucas, but she always took his feelings into consideration because he was her soul tie, and he'd always been in her heart. As much as Ava wanted to be a part of Frank-Lucas life, she knew Frank-Lucas was set in his ways. Deep down Ava wanted to see where things could go. But, she knew Frank-Lucas wasn't ready for that. How could he be ready or how could she be ready for something after just separating from Jack? Frank-Lucas was used to giving a little. He was very shut-down at times when it came to his feelings. Ava was the opposite of that. She loved love, and she wore her feelings on her sleeves. Frank-Lucas knew that Ava loved him unconditionally. She wanted to see them make it one day, but she knew she would have to either accept Frank-Lucas for who he was or move on from him. Hard as this decision was, Ava decided her and Frank-Lucas should be just friends. She accepted that from him because she cared for him, but she decided she wasn't giving him her attention, time, and love as she did once before.

Ava was used to living her life for many years without Frank-Lucas. She grew into this amazing woman who knew who she was and knew what she deserved. Ava struggled with her heart and mind when it came to Frank-Lucas, but she knew she deserved better than what he had to offer her. Her heart always got the best of her at first, but in the end, her mind always won. Ava made excuses for Frank-Lucas at times. She told herself that he was grieving the loss of his mom—that was why he was so shut-down at times—but honestly, this wasn't completely true for Frank-Lucas. Ava started to realize that Frank-Lucas was selfish, self-absorbed, and a low-key narcissist. Frank-Lucas didn't want to lose Ava because Ava brought light and value to his life, but Frank-Lucas depleted her soul. He drained the people who loved him and adored him the most. Ava felt drained at times when she dealt with Frank-Lucas. She would have to take time off from him to feel renewed again.

Ava didn't want that anymore. She desired more from him and needed him to fill her cup instead of drain it. Ava opened up to Frank-Lucas about this. He said he would do better, but he didn't. Ava even told him she was planning to go on a date with someone else. He said, "Please don't like him." Ava felt angry with him because he didn't say what she wanted him to say. She wanted Frank-Lucas to ask her on a date and do the things that other guys wanted to do with her. All he wanted was sex and a good meal. Ava was tired of that. Even though they only had sex a couple of times, she didn't want to have sex with him anymore. She wanted something from him that he couldn't offer her. Ava spoke with Frank-Lucas about his behavior and ways, and she demanded that he do better. Frank-Lucas hated when Ava would demand things from him. He felt he had no control over the situation when she did that. Ava didn't care anymore about his feelings. She was fed up with him and ready to have closure with him. Her plan was to give him exactly what he wanted for his birthday and then leave him alone. Well, she did just that. She asked him if he needed closure from her because she thought she needed it from him, but really she didn't. He gave her everything she needed the last night they spoke. Ava decided that was it. She was done with Frank-Lucas for real this time. This toxic love affair they'd endured for such a long time had to end for good.

Chapter 17

Ava woke up the next morning after seeing Frank-Lucas, and she felt relaxed and good. Ava finally felt empowered. She felt a sense of relief, almost like she dropped a whole person's worth of weight off her. In reality, she did. A part of her wanted to grieve the relationship (or "situation-ship") she and Frank-Lucas once shared, but the other part of her wanted to celebrate her sobriety. It was almost like she was a recovering alcoholic who was celebrating twenty years of recovery, but love was the case for Ava. She was celebrating her release of love for Frank-Lucas. Ava was celebrating her self-worth and her new profound sense of freedom from Frank-Lucas. Ava felt good about her decision when it came to letting Frank-Lucas go. She knew Frank-Lucas couldn't change for her. She knew that he was still the same little boy he was many years ago. Ava knew that she had to move forward so she wouldn't lose the wonderful and beautiful woman she had become. She had become all of this without Frank-Lucas, and if she had made things work long ago with him, she wouldn't be who she is today.

Like Ava, there are so many women who make themselves little so that they are able to stroke the egos of the men or the people they love. Ava started to realize that she was changing who she was again, just like she did with Jack. Ava didn't want to repeat her mistakes again. Furthermore, Frank-Lucas was a narcissistic, egoistic man-child. Ava didn't have time to read a book to Frank-Lucas and tell him he would be OK. She needed more in her life and required more from him. Ava loved Frank-Lucas and Jack, but she loved herself more. She respected both of them and what they brought to her life. She learned so much about herself through being in situations and relationships with both these men. She needed someone unlike Frank-Lucas or Jack who would put her first, of course after God. She wanted to feel like a priority in her man's life. Ava knew she was not going to be anyone's option but their first choice. Ava decided she wasn't going to settle for less anymore. Ava still cared for both Jack and Frank-Lucas but she desired so much more. Some would say Ava was too needy or that she was spoiled and selfish. This may have been the case but as an adult, Ava has the right to choose what is best for her life or who she feels deserve that spot or role in her life.

Ava is single and happy now. Ava loves the woman who she has become. She's happy with herself and her children. She's finally able to focus on what is important in her life, outside of loving a man, and that is her relationship with God, her children, her schooling, and her career. Ava is going out with her friends and she's living her life. Ava thought at first it was a mistake she made when she reconnected with Frank-Lucas, but it wasn't. It was apart of her story. It was a chapter in her life that she needed to go through. Ava was able to love four different times. If she was able to love four men in her life thus far, then there is definitely room for a fifth. Lastly, Ava still believes in love and one day finding that true person for her. In the meantime, Ava will live life and enjoy every moment of it!

THE END

ABOUT THE AUTHOR

Tameka Cummings was born April 19th, 1981 in South Carolina and raised in North Carolina. A wife and mother of three children, Tameka's background is in human services, mental health, and psychology and she is a small business owner. Tameka enjoys writing about the impact of imperfections and passions on love and relationships. She is excited for her debut publication, *Her Complicated Love*, to help others along their paths to loving themselves first. Her hope is that her daughter, her nieces, and other young girls who read her book can know how to choose themselves when it comes to love.

Printed in the USA
CPSIA information can be obtained
at www.ICGtesting.com
LVHW041245110823
754883LV00003B/722